COCONUT OIL

Jessica Oldfield
photography by Victoria Wall Harris

COCONUT OIL

hardie grant books

CONTENTS

HOW CAN I BENEFIT FROM USING COCONUT OIL?

Why is coconut oil a superfood?

It is a common misconception that coconut oil is bad for your health. Coconut oil is in fact a 'good' fat, containing a unique group of healthy saturated fats called Medium Chain Fatty Acids (MCFAs). Medium refers to the chain length of fatty acids and oils, which usually contain a mixture of short, medium and long chains. MCFAs are thought to have great health benefits.

For centuries, Asian, Indian and Polynesian communities have been using coconut oil as a nutritious food source and effective medicine. It forms a staple part of their diet and researchers have linked this with their low rates of heart disease, cancer and other degenerative diseases. The Western world is only just waking up to the health benefits of coconut oil and its impressive superfood status.

Health benefits

Although coconut oil is 92 percent saturated fat, the fats, or MCFAs, are broken down quickly and used predominately by the body to burn as fuel. They are not deposited as fat, unlike the Long Chain Fatty Acids (LCFAs) found in animal fats.

Unlike other plant-based and animal fats, coconut oil:

- protects against heart disease, cancer, diabetes and a host of other degenerative illnesses;
- supports and strengthens the immune system;
- promotes weight loss;
- aids digestion and improves mineral absorption;
- has germ-fighting, antibacterial properties when used topically.

The health benefits of coconut oil are due to a natural, miracle ingredient – lauric acid. Coconut oil is composed of about 48 percent lauric acid, a fatty acid with powerful anti-microbial properties that help the body to fight disease. Coconut oil is high in antioxidants, which help to lower inflammation in the body and also contain vitamins E and K as well as minerals such as iron.

Health professionals now consider coconut oil to be the healthiest oil we can use, and if part of a balanced diet, it can greatly benefit our health and wellbeing.

WHICH COCONUT OIL DO I CHOOSE?

Choosing which coconut oil to buy can seem overwhelming given the amount of choices now available. Most supermarkets have a good range, but there can be a big difference in price point and quality.

Although there are a variety of methods used to produce coconut oil, refined and virgin coconut oil are the two major categories.

Refined coconut oil

This oil, also known as refined, bleached and deodorised coconut oil, is usually extracted from dried coconut, known as copra, which is sun-dried, smoked or heated in a kiln. Copra-based oils are subjected to several refining processes to make it suitable for eating. It is 'bleached' using bleaching clay to remove impurities, then it is 'deodorised' using steam. The result is an often odourless coconut oil with a mild flavour. Some people prefer refined coconut oil for this reason, as it doesn't flavour food or scent the skin when used topically. The only refined coconut oil to avoid as a dietary oil is hydrogenated, which contains trans fats, but this is often used as an ingredient in cosmetics.

Virgin coconut oil

This oil is more expensive, typically less refined and therefore higher in antioxidants than refined coconut oil. It is also better quality as it is made from fresh coconut. Virgin oils characteristically have a stronger coconut taste and scent. While it is ideal to buy organic, it is not essential to ensure good-quality oil, as there are no genetically modified varieties of coconuts and very few pesticides are used on coconut trees.

Extraction methods

Once you have chosen either a refined or virgin coconut oil, you must then decide on an extraction method.

Common extraction methods used in both refined and virgin varieties include expeller-pressed and cold-pressed. Generally speaking, both methods produce healthy, flavoursome oil as they extract the oil from the seed using mechanical pressure, low temperatures and no chemicals. The best way to decide is to try a few different brands and find one that suits your budget, taste and use.

HOW DO I COOK WITH COCONUT OIL?

When choosing a nutritious oil to use in the kitchen, choose one that is healthy when used cold, at room temperature or after cooking. Coconut oil can be heated to 177°C/351°F without compromising its health properties. It is a stable oil, which means that it doesn't break down easily when heated or create harmful by-products like other vegetable oils can. This makes it an excellent choice for sautéing, roasting and even frying, as well as using cold in salad dressings, desserts and snacks.

As coconut oil is a semi-solid, highly saturated fat, it is the least susceptible out of all the dietary oils (animal and plant-based) to becoming rancid quickly and causing free radical damage when heated. Free radical damage is thought to be responsible for many health issues, such as arthritis and ageing, so when considering our health, it is one of the safest oils we can cook with.

Coconut oil can be substituted wherever an oil or fat is required. It is versatile both in flavour and its resistance to heat, so can be used to prepare meat, fish, vegetables and fruit from any cuisine.

Using other coconut products

Coconut milk, coconut cream and fresh and dried coconut are other versatile coconut products, which are included in this book and also contain the beneficial fatty acids. It is estimated that the following amounts of coconut oil and/or coconut products are to be consumed each day to achieve the recommended dietary intake of MCFAs necessary for optimal health*:

50 g pure coconut oil

150 g fresh coconut meat

80 g dried shredded coconut

295 ml coconut milk

The method for extracting coconut milk and cream from fresh coconut meat is explained on page 12, and used throughout the recipes, but canned coconut cream and milk can replace fresh in any of the recipes. The everyday recipes in this book are designed to help you conveniently add coconut oil to your diet. They are quick, healthy and delicious to ensure that you and your family get the health benefits of this miracle oil.

---

* Fife C.N., N.D., Bruce, *The Coconut Oil Miracle*

HOW TO EXTRACT COCONUT MEAT/CREAM/MILK

Extracting the white flesh, also known as the 'meat', from a fresh coconut or using it to produce coconut milk and cream may seem like a daunting task. However, it is a very simple process.

What are coconut cream and milk?

Coconut cream and milk are simply mixtures of fresh coconut meat and water combined and then squeezed out to produce 'milk'. Although the quality of canned coconut cream and milk has dramatically improved, there's nothing quite like the flavour or nutritional value of fresh coconut meat and milk.

How to extract coconut meat

When selecting a fresh coconut, always give it a good shake and choose one that has a lot of water inside. You want one with a maximum amount of juice.

1. Hold the coconut in the palm of your hand and position it over a sink with a bowl underneath to catch the water. With the back of the knife or cleaver strike the coconut in the centre. Repeat 2 or 3 times, rotating with each new strike. When the coconut cracks open catch the water in the bowl. You can use this coconut water when making coconut milk (see opposite) or drink it immediately; it's full of hydrating electrolytes.

2. Using a coconut scraper or a hand grater fastened to the work surface, grate the coconut meat from the shell one half at time, rotating the shell in the palm of your hand as you go. Once you have removed all the white meat from both halves of the coconut, discard the hard shell. At this stage the fresh coconut meat can be eaten raw or cooked. There are many suggestions of how to use fresh coconut meat in the recipes in this book.

How to make coconut cream and milk

1. For coconut cream and milk, place 150 g of the fresh grated coconut meat with 1 litre of filtered water in a blender. Blend on high until smooth, about 2–3 minutes.

2. Pour the mixture into a jug lined with a nut milk bag or piece of muslin. Squeeze the coconut mixture to extract as much liquid as possible into the jug below. This first extract, also known as coconut cream, contains more fat content then the second extract, also known as coconut milk.

For coconut milk, repeat the process, reusing the coconut meat. The cream and milk can be used straightaway, stored in the refrigerator for up to 4 days in an airtight container or frozen for up to 3 months.

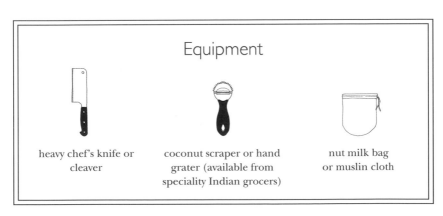

Equipment

| heavy chef's knife or cleaver | coconut scraper or hand grater (available from speciality Indian grocers) | nut milk bag or muslin cloth |

BASICS

These easy, dairy-free yoghurts, sauces and cheese are beautiful condiments to have on hand and will give any dish a boost of flavour, texture and coconut-oil goodness.

Coconut Yoghurt • Coconut Labne
Coconut Oil Mayonnaise • Coconut Oil Aioli

COCONUT YOGHURT

Makes: about 750 ml

YOU NEED
660 g coconut cream

probiotic powder from 2 probiotic capsules or 2 tablespoons shop-bought

1 tablespoon maple syrup (optional)

The probiotics in this yoghurt are great for digestive health.

D *Dairy-free* **D** *Aids digestion* **S** *Refined sugar-free*

Whisk the coconut cream and probiotic powder until smooth. Pour into a sterilised
jar and seal. Place in a warm, sunny place for 12 hours, then chill overnight.
Alternatively, use a yoghurt-maker. Blend the mixture in a food processor with
maple syrup, if using, until smooth. Return to the jar and seal. It will thicken in the
refrigerator. Store for 3 weeks.

COCONUT LABNE

Makes: about 500 g

YOU NEED

500 g Coconut Yoghurt (see page 16) or shop bought, stirred to combine any liquid
that has separated out • 2 tablespoons lemon juice • 1 teaspoon salt

Labne contains probiotics to help keep the digestive system healthy.

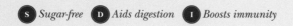

S *Sugar-free*   **D** *Aids digestion*   **I** *Boosts immunity*

Pour the yoghurt through a muslin-lined sieve set over a bowl. Add the lemon juice and salt. Gather the sides of the muslin together and tie a knot in the top. Press the parcel into the sieve, releasing the liquid into the bowl. Weigh down, then chill for 12 hours. Unwrap: it should be soft, but firm enough to hold its shape. Squeeze out the liquid and drain if necessary. To store, break off a piece, roll into a small ball then put into a sterilised jar. Repeat. Cover with olive oil and chill until ready to eat.

COCONUT OIL MAYONNAISE

Makes: about 500 g

YOU NEED

1 free-range egg yolk • 2 teaspoons Dijon mustard • 250 ml coconut oil, melted

1 tablespoon apple cider vinegar • 1 tablespoon lemon juice • 1 teaspoon salt

Contains good fats to help protect against heart disease as well as antioxidants and minerals to strengthen the immune system.

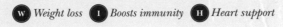

W *Weight loss* I *Boosts immunity* H *Heart support*

Place the egg yolk and mustard in a bowl and start to whisk in the oil, bit by bit, until it starts to thicken. Add the vinegar, then pour in the remaining oil in a thin, steady stream, whisking vigorously to combine. Add the lemon juice and salt and whisk to combine. Chill for up to a week. If the mayo solidifies, place in a mug of hot water to return it to the desired consistency.

COCONUT OIL AIOLI

Makes: about 250 ml

YOU NEED
1 small garlic clove • 1 teaspoon salt • 1 free-range egg yolk

1 teaspoon Dijon mustard • 250 ml coconut oil, melted

2 tablespoons lemon juice • ¼ teaspoon cracked pepper

Garlic has many nutritional and medicinal properties, especially when eaten raw, as it can help fight infection.

H *Heart support*   **A** *Antiviral*   **C** *Lowers cholesterol*

Mash the garlic with the salt in a mortar and pestle. Place the egg yolk and mustard in a bowl and start to whisk in the oil, bit by bit, until it starts to thicken. Add the lemon juice, then pour in the remaining oil in a thin, steady stream, whisking vigorously to combine. Add the garlic and pepper and whisk to combine. Chill for up to 1 week.

BREAKFAST

Whether you have slow-paced mornings or are always in a rush, there's a breakfast in this chapter to suit everyone's schedule. Protein-packed pancakes to keep you satisfied, a quick, nutrient-packed smoothie you can run out the door with and make-ahead chia puddings high in omega-3 for optimal brain function.

Breakfast Smoothie • Coconut Fruit Salad
Buckwheat Pancakes with Banana
Coconut Granola • Coconut & Chocolate Toast
Scrambled Eggs on Sourdough
Chia Seed Breakfast Pudding

BREAKFAST SMOOTHIE

Serves: 1

YOU NEED

1 medium banana • 70 g ice cubes • 1 medium passion fruit

2–3 black kale leaves, stems removed • 1 cinnamon stick, crumbled

2½ tablespoons Coconut Yoghurt (see page 16 or use store-bought)

1 teaspoon chia seeds • 2 teaspoons brown rice syrup

This smoothie is a great nutrient booster as the chia seeds contain healthy omega-3 fatty acids, while kale has lots of vitamins and minerals to help get rid of toxins.

A *Alkalising*   **A** *Anti-inflammatory*   **B** *Brain support*

Blend all of the ingredients with 60 ml of water in a high-speed blender until completely smooth. Pour into a glass and enjoy.

COCONUT FRUIT SALAD

Serves: 1

YOU NEED

30 g flaked almonds • 45 g fresh coconut, finely grated

1 banana, peeled and cut into large chunks

100 g kiwi fruit, peeled and cut into wedges • ½ passion fruit (about 50 g)

1½ teaspoons honey • 40 g raspberries

Kiwi and passion fruit contain vitamin C to fight infections, while banana is a good source of potassium and almonds are high in protein.

E *Energising*　**H** *Heart support*　**I** *Boosts immunity*

Dry-fry the almonds for 3–4 minutes until golden. Cool completely. Spread the coconut evenly onto a plate. Toss half of the banana and half of the kiwi in the coconut to coat. Place the passion fruit in the centre of a serving plate. Arrange the banana pieces around the passion fruit in an alternating pattern. Arrange the kiwi in the same way. Drizzle honey over the top and scatter with almonds and raspberries.

BUCKWHEAT PANCAKES WITH BANANA

Serves: 1 (makes 2–3 pancakes)

YOU NEED
1 egg • 120 ml milk • 2 teaspoons coconut oil, melted • 40 g buckwheat flour
40 g spelt or plain flour • ¼ teaspoon salt • ½ teaspoon baking powder
1 banana, peeled and thinly sliced • 1 tablespoon pure maple syrup

Buckwheat is packed with zinc, copper and manganese to help build cells, keep the cardiovascular system healthy and stabilise blood sugar levels.

D *Aids digestion*   **I** *Boosts immunity*   **B** *Lowers blood pressure*

Whisk the egg, milk and half of the oil together. In another bowl, combine the flours, salt and baking powder. Add the wet ingredients to the dry and stir until combined. Heat a frying pan over a medium to high heat. Drizzle the remaining oil over the base of the pan. Ladle a scoop of the batter into the pan, rotating the pan to bring the batter to the edges. Lay the banana slices on top and cook for 1–2 minutes until bubbles appear on the surface and the pancake is golden. Flip and cook for 1 minute. Repeat. Stack pancakes. Drizzle with maple syrup.

COCONUT GRANOLA

Makes: about 500 g

YOU NEED

350 g rolled oats (or quinoa flakes for gluten-free option)

200 g whole raw almonds, roughly chopped • 80 g pumpkin seeds

50 g unsweetened coconut flakes • 125 ml coconut oil, melted

5 tablespoons (100 g) pure maple syrup or rice malt syrup

½ teaspoon salt • 150 g currants

The nuts and seeds in this refined-sugar-free granola are high in protein and fibre.

B *Builds bones*   **E** *Energising*   **H** *Heart support*

Preheat the oven to 180°C/350°F/Gas 4. Line a baking tray with baking paper.
Combine the rolled oats, almonds, pumpkin seeds and coconut flakes. Heat the oil,
maple syrup and salt gently until just melted. Pour over the oat mixture and mix
well. Spread the mixture over a baking tray and bake for 10 minutes, then stir in the
currants. Bake for 10–15 minutes until golden. Cool on a tray.
Store in an airtight container for 2 weeks.

COCONUT & CHOCOLATE TOAST

Serves: 1–2

YOU NEED

2 slices seeded sourdough bread • 1 teaspoon coconut oil

½ teaspoon honey • small pinch of salt

¼ teaspoon raw cacao powder • 15 raspberries

Raspberries contain high levels of antioxidants, honey is a great antibacterial to help the digestive system and cacao is rich in magnesium.

A *Antibacterial* **D** *Aids digestion* **A** *Anti-inflammatory*

Toast the sourdough. Spread over the coconut oil, followed by the honey. Sprinkle over the salt. Dust with cacao powder and top with crushed raspberries.

SCRAMBLED EGGS ON SOURDOUGH

Serves: 1

YOU NEED
3 eggs • ⅛ teaspoon salt • pinch of ground turmeric

6 cherry tomatoes, quartered • ½ teaspoon coconut oil

1 slice sourdough bread, toasted • pinch of freshly ground black pepper

Turmeric has powerful nutritional benefits as it contains a compound called curcumin, which has insulin moderating effects on the body.

D *Detoxifying*   **A** *Anti-inflammatory*   **B** *Stabilises blood sugar*

Whisk the eggs, salt and turmeric together. Add the tomatoes and combine. Gently heat the oil in a frying pan. When the oil has melted, add the eggs and stir gently from the edges to the centre of the pan. Cook, stirring, until the eggs look glossy but still slightly underdone. Remove from the heat and let the heat of the pan finish cooking the eggs. Pile the eggs on top of the toast and season with pepper.

CHIA SEED BREAKFAST PUDDING

Makes: 500 ml

YOU NEED

1 tablespoon coconut oil • 1 teaspoon vanilla extract • 2 tablespoons honey
500 ml almond milk • 45 g black or white chia seeds
1 medium peach, chopped into bite-sized chunks • 100 g blueberries

Chia seeds are high in omega-3 fatty acids, while almond milk is a great plant-based protein and peach is a rich source of folate.

D *Detoxifying*   **A** *Anti-inflammatory*   **H** *Heart support*

Blend the oil, vanilla, honey and almond milk in a high-speed blender until smooth. Pour into a bowl and whisk in the chia seeds to avoid clumping. Chill overnight, then whisk to loosen the mixture – it should have a thick, pudding-like texture. Place a spoonful of the mixture in a 500 ml jar, then add a layer of peach and blueberries on top. Repeat, layering to top of jar.

MAINS

These delicious, mostly whole food recipes are perfect for weeknights or weekends. Using simple ingredients to create spritely dressed salads, heart-warming curries and satisfying soups, these dishes can be served independently as meals or mix and match them for multiple course menus.

Fish Baked in Fresh Coconut
Leek Risotto with Mushrooms
Braised Chard with Bacon • Fennel Slaw with
Smoked Salmon • Spaghetti with Coconut
Prawns • Potato & Coconut Dauphinoise
Pumpkin with Coconut Polenta • Broccoli Salad
with Coconut Labne • Leek, Sweet Potato
& Coconut Soup • Tomato & Apple Soup with
Feta • British India Sandwich • Dhal with Crispy
Onion • Fish Curry • Lentil, Tomato & Herb Salad
Quinoa Nasi Goreng • Beef & Crunchy Salad
Salmon with Broccolini • Coconut Carbonara
Lamb with Beans & Hazelnuts
Chicken with Coconut Gremolata

FISH BAKED IN FRESH COCONUT

Serves: 2

YOU NEED

45 g plain flour • ¾ teaspoon salt • 60 g fresh coconut meat or equal amount
of dried coconut rehydrated in water for 20 minutes then drained
2 × 200 g perch or other white fish fillets • 1 egg, lightly beaten
large bunch of kale (about 200 g), leaves removed and roughly chopped
juice from ½ large lemon

White fish is a great source of omega-3 fatty acids, while kale is packed with fibre, potassium, vitamin C and vitamin B6, which is good for the heart.

F *High fibre*   **H** *Heart support*   **B** *Brain support*

Preheat the oven to 200°C/400°F/Gas 6. Line a baking tray with baking paper. Sift the flour and ½ teaspoon of the salt onto a plate. Spread the coconut out onto another plate. Lightly coat both sides of the fish in flour. Dip the fish in the egg, then coat in the coconut. Put the fish on a baking tray and bake for 10 minutes until golden. Flip and bake for a further 10 minutes. Blanch the kale for 60 seconds until bright green. Plunge into iced water. Remove and season with the remaining salt and the lemon juice. Serve the fish on top of the kale with a slice of lemon.

LEEK RISOTTO WITH MUSHROOMS

Serves: 4

YOU NEED
1.2 litres vegetable stock • 2 tablespoons coconut oil
1 large leek, chopped • 330 g arborio rice • ½ teaspoon salt
500 g Portobello mushrooms, sliced • 150 g shaved Parmesan cheese

Mushrooms contain high iron levels and are a rich source of calcium, which is an essential nutrient in the formation and strength of bones.

B *Lowers blood pressure*   **I** *Boosts immunity*   **B** *Strengthens bones*

Heat the stock until nearly boiling, then keep on a very low simmer. Heat 1 tablespoon of the oil in a pan over a low heat. Fry the leek for 10 minutes until soft and translucent. Increase the heat to medium, add the rice and salt and stir. Cook for 1 minute. Add 1 ladleful of stock and stir until the liquid is absorbed. Continue to add ladlefuls of stock, one at a time, until the rice is cooked, which should take about 30 minutes. Brush the remaining oil onto a griddle pan and grill the mushrooms until golden. Take the risotto off the heat and stir in the Parmesan and most of the mushrooms. Serve the risotto with the reserved mushrooms sprinkled on top.

BRAISED CHARD WITH BACON

Serves: 4 as a side

YOU NEED

1 tablespoon coconut oil • 1 large leek, sliced into rings
2 large bunches rainbow chard, leaves and stalks roughly chopped
4 rashers rindless bacon, roughly chopped • 180 ml white wine
180 g cooked chickpeas • ¼ teaspoon salt

Bacon and chickpeas are packed with protein to help our bodies repair cells and maintain good muscle health.

F *High fibre*   **E** *Energising*   **M** *Builds muscle*

Heat the oil in a pan and gently fry the leek and chard stalks for 10 minutes, stirring occasionally, until soft and translucent. Increase the heat to medium, add the bacon and fry for 4–5 minutes until the edges are crisp and golden. Add the chard leaves and stir for 1 minute until slightly wilted. Pour in the wine and stir for 2–3 minutes until evaporated. Add the chickpeas and salt. Stir and serve.

FENNEL SLAW WITH SMOKED SALMON

Serves: 4 as a side

YOU NEED

50 g coconut cream • juice of 1 lemon • 15 g dill, leaves picked and finely chopped
1 large fennel bulb, thinly shaved • 250 g smoked salmon, torn into large pieces
150 g Jarlsberg cheese, thinly shaved • 1 teaspoon capers

Fennel is high in fibre and vitamin C and can cleanse and protect the liver from harmful chemicals. Smoked salmon is rich in omega-3 to boost brain function.

L *Cleanses liver*   **F** *High fibre*   **B** *Brain support*

Whisk together the coconut cream, lemon juice and dill to make the dressing. Set aside. Arrange the fennel on a plate, spreading it out to the edges. Follow with the salmon, then the Jarlsberg cheese. Using a spoon, drizzle the dressing over the salad. Scatter the capers over the top.

SPAGHETTI WITH COCONUT PRAWNS

Serves: 2

YOU NEED
250 g dried spaghetti

1 tablespoon coconut oil • 12 raw prawns (about 250 g), deveined and peeled,
with tails intact (heads and shells reserved), rinsed • 2 garlic cloves, crushed
2 long red chillies, thinly sliced on the diagonal (reserving a handful to garnish)
2 tablespoons tomato purée • ½ teaspoon salt • 150 g fresh coconut
or equal amount of dried coconut rehydrated in water for 20 minutes then drained

Prawns are a great source of protein and zinc while chilli is rich in vitamin C and beta-carotene, which helps to improve the body's defences.

A *Anti-inflammatory*   **B** *Bone building*   **I** *Boosts immunity*

Cook the spaghetti. Drain, reserving 125 ml of water. Heat ½ tablespoon of oil, add the prawn shells and heads and press down, releasing the juices. Add the water and simmer until the water turns light orange. Strain, discard the shells and reserve the stock. Heat the remaining oil and fry the garlic and chillies for 1 minute. Add the prawns and sauté for 1 minute. Add the tomato purée and stock and simmer for a few minutes. Add the spaghetti, salt and coconut. Toss, adding the pasta water, if needed. Top with the reserved chilli.

POTATO & COCONUT DAUPHINOISE

Serves: 4

YOU NEED

1 kg Desiree or other starchy potatoes, unpeeled and thinly sliced

300 ml coconut cream • 1 red onion, sliced • 2 garlic cloves, crushed

2 teaspoons cracked black pepper • 1 teaspoon salt

4 thyme sprigs, leaves picked and chopped • 50 g Cheddar cheese, grated

Cheese is an important source of calcium, while coconut cream is a great source of healthy fats for the heart.

F *High fibre*   **B** *Strengthens bones*   **H** *Heart support*

Preheat the oven to 220°C/425°F/Gas 7. Place the potatoes, coconut cream, ½ of the onion, the garlic, pepper and salt into an ovenproof baking dish and toss to combine. Put on the stove over a medium heat, pour in 200 ml of boiling water, then cover tightly with 2 layers of foil. Cook for 10–15 minutes until the potatoes are soft when pressed but not falling apart. Uncover, scatter the remaining onion, cheese and thyme over the top and cook in the oven for 15 minutes until golden.

PUMPKIN WITH COCONUT POLENTA

Serves: 4

YOU NEED

1 kg kabocha or pumpkin, cut into 4 large wedges, deseeded, skin left on

2 tablespoons tamari • 1 tablespoon coconut oil, melted

3 garlic cloves, crushed • 800 ml canned or fresh coconut milk

180 g polenta • 2 teaspoons parsley leaves, chopped

Polenta is high in beta-carotene, which is converted into vitamin A for healthy skin and is a great source of dietary fibre.

 High-fibre   **B** _Blood sugar control_   **S** _Boosts skin_

Preheat the oven to 200°C/400°F/Gas 6. Line an ovenproof dish with baking paper. Prick the pumpkin with a fork and place it in a dish. Whisk together the tamari, oil, 4 tablespoons of water and the garlic. Massage this mixture into the pumpkin. Cover with baking paper and roast for 30–40 minutes until tender but not mushy. Mix the coconut milk with 200 ml of water in a pan and bring to the boil, then simmer and pour in the polenta, whisking. Reduce the heat to low and whisk for 10 minutes until thick. Sprinkle with the parsley. Serve the polenta with the roasted pumpkin.

BROCCOLI SALAD WITH COCONUT LABNE

Serves: 4

YOU NEED

35 g flaked almonds • 1 tablespoon coconut oil

2 heads of broccoli including stalks (about 650 g), broken into small florets

and stalks thinly sliced into 5 mm rounds • 2 garlic cloves

1 teaspoon salt • 10 dried dates, finely sliced

40 g Coconut Labne, torn (see page 18) • 2 teaspoons orange blossom water

Broccoli is a powerful source of antioxidants and vitamins that nourish the body, while almonds are excellent brain food and help repair weak memory.

F *High-fibre*   **A** *Anti-inflammatory*   **B** *Brain support*

Dry-fry the almonds in a frying pan over a medium heat for 2–3 minutes until golden. Set aside. Heat the oil in a frying pan over a high heat. Toss in the broccoli stalks and fry for 1 minute. Add the florets and fry for another minute. Reduce the heat to medium, add the garlic and salt and mix. Fry for 5–6 minutes until the florets turn bright green and the stalks are tender. Spread the broccoli over a plate. Cool slightly, then sprinkle with the orange blossom water, and scatter with the dates, labne and almonds.

LEEK, SWEET POTATO & COCONUT SOUP

Serves: 4

YOU NEED
1 tablespoon coconut oil • 1 large leek, chopped

3–4 sweet potatoes (about 600 g), peeled and chopped • 1.25 litres vegetable stock

1 teaspoon salt • 110 g canned or fresh coconut milk • 10 g parsley leaves, chopped

Coconut milk is rich in antioxidants that fight toxins in the body and prevent free radicals. Sweet potato contains essential vitamins and minerals to boost metabolism.

D *Dairy-free*　**A** *Anti-inflammatory*　**M** *Boosts metabolism*

Heat the oil over a low heat. Fry the leek for 10 minutes until soft and translucent. Add the sweet potatoes, stock and salt. Bring to the boil, then simmer for 10–15 minutes until the sweet potato is soft and collapses when pressed with back of spoon. Take off the heat and purée with a hand-held blender until smooth. Return to the heat, add the coconut milk and gently heat through. Garnish with the parsley.

TOMATO & APPLE SOUP WITH FETA

Serves: 4

YOU NEED

1 kg large vine-ripened tomatoes, halved • 4 large Granny Smith apples
(about 500 g total), peeled, cored and chopped • 3 tablespoons coconut oil, melted
1 teaspoon fennel seeds • 1 red chilli, deseeded (optional) and finely chopped
1 litre vegetable stock • freshly ground black pepper • 50 g feta cheese

Fennel seeds contain many beneficial, cancer-fighting antioxidants, while tomatoes also help fight off diseases and reduces the risk of heart disease.

B *Builds bones* **I** *Fights infection* **H** *Heart support*

Preheat the oven to 180°C/350°F/Gas 4. Line a baking dish with baking paper. Put the tomatoes and apples in a single layer in the dish. Drizzle over 2 tablespoons of oil. Bake for 40–45 minutes until very soft and golden at the edges. Cool slightly. Process the mixture in the blender with any juices in 2 batches. Heat the remaining oil over a medium heat. Fry the fennel seeds and chilli, if using, for 1 minute until fragrant. Add the tomato mixture and stock and simmer for 10 minutes. Season with pepper. Top with the crumbled feta.

BRITISH INDIA SANDWICH

Serves: 2

YOU NEED

½ teaspoon coconut oil • 100 g paneer cheese, thinly sliced

2 shop-bought naan breads • 1 tablespoon Coconut Oil Aioli (see page 22)

30 g baby spinach • 10 g coriander leaves • juice of ½ lemon

Coconut and fresh coriander both have many curative properties and are particularly effective in lowering bad cholesterol.

B *Builds bones*   **B** *Blood sugar control*   **H** *Heart support*

Heat the oil in a frying pan over a medium to high heat. Add the paneer and fry for 2–3 minutes until golden on both sides. Set aside. Wipe the pan clean, return to a medium heat and dry-fry the naans in batches for 1–2 minutes each side.
To assemble, spread the aioli over one side of the naan, going right to the edges. Place the spinach, paneer and coriander onto half of the naan. Squeeze over the lemon juice, then fold over the other half of the naan.

DHAL WITH CRISPY ONION

Serves: 4

YOU NEED

2 tablespoons coconut oil • 10 curry leaves • 5 garlic cloves, chopped

10 cm piece of ginger, peeled and finely grated • 2 red onions, sliced

1 tablespoon curry powder • 1 teaspoon salt

250 g red lentils, soaked in cold water for 20 minutes then drained

400 ml canned or fresh coconut milk

Spices such as coriander, turmeric and ginger have many medicinal properties, such as immunity and digestive support.

D *Aids digestion*   **A** *Anti-inflammatory*   **I** *Boosts immunity*

Heat 1 tablespoon of the oil in a pan over a medium to high heat. Add the curry leaves and fry for 1 minute. Add the garlic, ginger, 1 sliced onion, curry powder and salt and fry for 3–4 minutes until fragrant. Add the lentils, coconut milk and 250 ml of water. Bring to the boil, then simmer for 15 minutes until the lentils are soft and the dhal has thickened. Heat the remaining oil in another pan over a high heat, add the remaining onion and fry until crispy. Drain.
Serve the dhal topped with crispy onion.

FISH CURRY

Serves: 4

YOU NEED

3 garlic cloves • 1 teaspoon salt • 2 tablespoons coconut oil

15 curry leaves, plus a few extra to garnish • 1 large onion, chopped

600 ml canned or fresh coconut milk • 60 g tamarind purée

4 mackerel fillets or other white fish fillets (about 200 g each)

Fish is full of heart-friendly omega-3 fatty acids, while tamarind, an ancient medicinal fruit, is known to lower cholesterol and help digestion.

D *Aids digestion* **H** *Heart support* **C** *Lowers cholesterol*

Crush the garlic with ½ teaspoon of the salt. Heat 1 tablespoon of the oil and fry the curry leaves for 1 minute. Add the garlic and onion and fry for 3–5 minutes until the onion turns golden. Add the milk and the remaining salt. Bring to the boil. Simmer for 15–20 minutes until thick. Turn off the heat and stir in the tamarind. Cover. Heat the remaining oil. Fry fish for 6–8 minutes until golden on each side. Top with the curry leaves. Serve with curry sauce.

LENTIL, TOMATO & HERB SALAD

Serves: 4 as a side

YOU NEED

250 g cherry tomatoes • 2 tablespoons coconut oil, plus 1 teaspoon

¼ teaspoon salt, plus extra • 250 g green lentils

2½ tablespoons white balsamic vinegar

20 g dill, finely chopped • 20 g mint, finely chopped

Lentils provide large amounts of folate, which is a big contributor to heart health, and dietary fibre, which assists digestive health and stabilises blood sugar levels.

D *Aids digestion*   **H** *Heart support*   **B** *Stabilises blood sugar*

Preheat the grill to high. Line a shallow baking tray with baking paper. Put the tomatoes, 1 teaspoon of the oil and ¼ teaspoon of the salt in the baking tray and mix. Grill for 7–8 minutes until the tomatoes blister and blacken. Cool. Cook the lentils in a pan of water with a few pinches of salt for 20 minutes until just soft. Drain and cool. To make the dressing, whisk together the remaining 2 tablespoons of the oil, the vinegar and the remaining salt. Combine the lentils, tomatoes and herbs. Pour over the dressing and mix.

QUINOA NASI GORENG

Serves: 4

YOU NEED

1 tablespoon coconut oil • 2 spring onions, sliced on a diagonal
(reserving a handful to garnish) • 2 garlic cloves, crushed
6 baby bok choy • 400 g tricoloured quinoa
2 tablespoons kecap manis (sweet soy sauce) • 1 tablespoon lemon juice

Quinoa is a complete protein, containing all 9 essential amino acids; it's rich in magnesium, which helps maintain healthy blood vessels.

F *High-fibre*   **H** *Heart support*   **A** *Anti-inflammatory*

Heat the oil over a medium to high heat. Fry the spring onions and garlic for 30 seconds. Add the bok choy and fry for 1 minute. Add the quinoa, kecap manis and 60 ml of water and simmer until most of the liquid has evaporated. Take off the heat and stir in the lemon juice. Serve, garnished with the reserved spring onions.

BEEF & CRUNCHY SALAD

Serves: 2

YOU NEED
2 sirloin steaks (about 250 g each) • ¼ teaspoon salt, plus an extra pinch
1 teaspoon coconut oil • ½ large Chinese cabbage (about 600 g)
1 small carrot, shredded • 100 g mangetout, tops, tails and strings
removed, but left whole • 15 g mint leaves, roughly torn • juice of 1 lime

This dish is an energy booster – the carrot and cabbage are rich in vitamin C, which helps our bodies absorb the high amounts of iron found in red meat.

E *Energising* **F** *High-fibre* **I** *Boosts immunity*

Season both sides of each sirloin with salt. Brush a large griddle pan with half of the oil over a medium to high heat. Fry the sirloins for 5–6 minutes each side, turning once until seared on both sides and pink in the middle. Rest for 5 minutes before cutting into thick slices. Combine the cabbage, carrot, mangetout and mint in a bowl. Whisk together the remaining oil, lime juice and salt. Arrange the sliced sirloin on plates with the salad and drizzle with dressing.

SALMON WITH BROCCOLINI

Serves: 2

YOU NEED

2 salmon fillets (about 100 g each), pat dry with kitchen paper and skin scored

1½ tablespoons sweet miso paste • 1 tablespoon mirin (rice wine)

½ teaspoon coconut oil, plus ½ tablespoon • 1 garlic clove, sliced

200 g broccolini • juice of ½ lemon

Miso paste contains a variety of beneficial disease-fighting nutrients. As a fermented food, it contains important probiotics for a healthy immune system.

D *Aids digestion* **H** *Heart support* **I** *Boosts immunity*

Put the fish in a container. Whisk the miso and mirin together, then pour over the salmon, tossing to coat. Cover and chill for 10 minutes. Heat ½ teaspoon of the oil and fry the fish for 2–3 minutes until golden. Flip and cook for 2–3 minutes. Rest for 5 minutes. Heat the remaining oil and fry the garlic for 30 seconds. Add the broccolini and fry for 6–7 minutes until bright green. Turn off the heat and add the lemon juice. Serve with the fish.

COCONUT CARBONARA

Serves: 2

YOU NEED

200 g dried spaghetti • ½ tablespoon coconut oil

225 g mixed mushrooms (enoki, oyster, Portobello, shiitake) • 1 egg yolk

75 ml coconut cream • 75 g Parmesan, grated, plus extra for sprinkling

½ teaspoon freshly cracked black pepper • 10 g parsley leaves, roughly chopped

Mushrooms are the only plant-based source of vitamin B12, making them an important energy food for vegans and vegetarians.

E *Energising*   **B** *Builds bones*   **I** *Boosts immunity*

Cook the spaghetti until al dente. Drain and reserve 125 ml of the cooking water. Heat the oil in a pan and sauté the mushrooms for 5–6 minutes until golden. Set aside. Lightly whisk the egg yolk, then add the coconut cream, Parmesan, pepper and parsley and whisk until combined. Add the fried mushrooms and mix. Heat through the cooked pasta. Turn off the heat and stir the sauce through the pasta, adding a little of the reserved water to loosen if needed. Sprinkle with Parmesan.

LAMB WITH BEANS & HAZELNUTS

Serves: 2

YOU NEED

6 lamb cutlets (about 400 g) • ½ teaspoon salt • 15 g sumac

1 tablespoon coconut oil • 1 garlic clove, crushed

220 g green beans, topped, tailed and strings removed

40 g hazelnuts, roughly chopped

Green beans are full of antioxidants to cleanse and detoxify the body. Lamb is a lean protein and hazelnuts are rich in B vitamins, which are vital for energy.

E *Energising*   **D** *Detoxifying*   **N** *Boosts nervous system*

Season both sides of the cutlets with ¼ teaspoon of the salt. Combine the sumac and ½ tablespoon of the oil, then massage into the cutlets. Leave for 10 minutes. Heat a griddle pan over a medium to high heat. Grill the cutlets for 2–3 minutes on each side until seared on the outside but pink in the middle. Rest for 5 minutes. Heat the remaining oil over a high heat. Fry the garlic for 30 seconds, then the add the beans and stir. Cook for 3–4 minutes until the beans are tender.

Add the hazelnuts and remaining salt and serve.

CHICKEN WITH COCONUT GREMOLATA

Serves: 4

YOU NEED

1.6 kg whole chicken

2 tablespoons lemon juice (reserving leftover lemon for the cavity of the chicken)

1 teaspoon salt • 1 tablespoon coconut oil

Gremolata

35 g freshly grated coconut or equal amount of dried
coconut rehydrated in water for 20 minutes then drained • 1 tablespoon parsley
leaves, finely chopped • 1 teaspoon grated lemon zest
1 garlic clove, minced

Parsley is high in vitamin C and iron and is used raw in this dish for optimum
nutrition and flavour, while chicken is high in protein.

I *Infection fighting*   **B** *Blood pressure control*   **I** *Boosts immunity*

Preheat the oven to 240°C/450°F/Gas 9. Line a baking dish with baking paper. Put
the chicken in the dish and prick all over with a fork. Massage the salt and oil into
the skin. Stuff the leftover lemon into the cavity. Put the chicken into the oven, then
reduce the temperature to 200°C/400°F/Gas 6. Roast for 50–60 minutes until the
internal temperature of the chicken reads 74°C/165°F and the juices run clear.
Mix the gremolata ingredients together. Pour the lemon juice over the chicken
and serve with gremolata.

SNACKS

There are always moments between meals
where you need to fill a gap.
These wholesome tarts, chips and dips
will ensure you always have tasty,
well-considered snacks on hand, which
makes avoiding unhealthy ones a
whole lot easier.

Pineapple Salad with Chilli • Fried Coconut, Nuts & Seeds • Coconut Chips • Cauliflower Bowl Mini Cauliflower & Cheese Tarts • Almond & Brazil Nut Butter • Crispy Tofu Coconut Guacamole • Bacon, Banana & Coconut Bagel • Potatoes with Coconut Yoghurt Beetroot Chips with Feta & Mint • Sweet Potato & Leek Quesadilla • Lime Prawns with Macadamia Crumb • Chargrilled Miso Corn

PINEAPPLE SALAD WITH CHILLI

Serves: 3–4

YOU NEED

½ pineapple (about 700 g), skin and core removed, cut into long pieces

1 handful of mint leaves • 1 teaspoon coconut oil, melted

½ teaspoon salt • ¼ teaspoon chilli flakes

Pineapple is high in potassium, which has been proven to lower blood pressure and is a fantastic source of vitamin C and fibre.

D *Aids digestion*　**I** *Fights infection*　**B** *Lowers blood pressure*

Put the pineapple in a bowl and add the coconut oil, salt and chilli flakes. Toss to coat. Arrange the pineapple on a plate and scatter with mint leaves.

FRIED COCONUT, NUTS & SEEDS

Serves: 2–3

YOU NEED

190 g raw almonds • 170 g raw cashew nuts • 35 g coconut chips

40 g pumpkin seeds • 2 teaspoons curry powder • 1 teaspoon salt

1 tablespoon coconut oil, melted

The combination of nuts and seeds make this an energy-boosting snack. Nuts and seeds are full of fibre, protein and essential fatty acids for optimum health.

F *High-fibre*   **B** *Builds bones*   **H** *Heart support*

Preheat the oven to 180°C/350°F/Gas 4. Line a baking tray with baking paper. Fry the curry powder in a dry pan over a medium to high heat for 2–3 minutes. Put the curry powder and other dry ingredients into a bowl and mix. Pour over the oil and work the oil through the mixture to coat. Spread the mixture onto a tray in an even layer. Roast for 20–30 minutes until golden all over, turning the mixture every 10–15 minutes.

COCONUT CHIPS

Serves: 2–3

YOU NEED
1 coconut • ½ tablespoon apple cider vinegar • ¼ teaspoon salt

This snack made from fresh coconut meat is full of health benefits. Its mineral levels of iron, zinc and phosphorous are high, it's full of fibre and contains good fats.

F *High-fibre* **H** *Heart support* **C** *Lowers cholesterol*

Preheat the oven to 180°C/350°F/Gas 4. Using a metal skewer, pierce 2 of the coconut eyes. Empty out and discard the water. Bake the coconut for 30 minutes until the shell begins to crack. Cool completely. Leave the oven on. Wrap the coconut in a cloth and hit several times with hammer to break up into large pieces. Separate the flesh from the shell and remove the outer skin with a vegetable peeler. Peel strips from each chunk. Toss in the vinegar and salt to coat. Bake for 10 minutes until toasted.

CAULIFLOWER BOWL

Serves: 1–2

YOU NEED

½ head cauliflower (about 230 g), broken into mini florets

1 tablespoon coconut oil, melted • 1 teaspoon cumin seeds

1 teaspoon salt • ½ teaspoon sweet (dulce) smoked paprika

½ teaspoon cracked black pepper • 1 tablespoon lemon juice

Cauliflower contains a high amount of vitamin C and choline, a B vitamin responsible for healthy brain development.

B *Brain support*   **I** *Fights infection*   **D** *Detoxifying*

Preheat the oven to 200°C/400°F/Gas 6. Line a baking tray with baking paper. Mix all of the ingredients, except the lemon juice, together in a bowl with your hands. Spread out in a single layer on the tray, then bake for 15–20 minutes until the cauliflower is golden and the edges are crisp. Drizzle the lemon juice over the cauliflower and serve.

MINI CAULIFLOWER & CHEESE TARTS

Makes: 12 mini tarts

YOU NEED

2 sheets shortcrust pastry • 80 g cauliflower, broken into 5 cm florets

1 egg, lightly beaten • 70 g Cheddar cheese, grated

60 ml coconut milk • 1 tablespoon coconut cream • ½ teaspoon salt

4 thyme sprigs, leaves picked and finely chopped (reserving a handful to garnish)

Thyme is a powerful detoxing herb, full of antioxidants that boost the immune system and is a great liver-cleansing food.

D *Detoxifying* **A** *Antiviral* **L** *Cleanses liver*

Line a 12-hole mini muffin tray with baking paper. Cut out 12 circles, slightly bigger than the holes of the tin, from the pastry and use to line each hole. Chill for 15 minutes, then prick the bases. Preheat the oven to 180°C/350°F/Gas 4. Blind bake the pastry for 10 minutes. Uncover and bake for 2–3 minutes until golden. Cool. Blanch the cauliflower for 60 seconds. Drain and cool. Whisk together the egg, cheese, milk, cream, salt and thyme. Divide the filling among the cases. Top with cauliflower. Sprinkle with the reserved thyme and bake for 15–20 minutes. Cool for 5 minutes.

ALMOND & BRAZIL NUT BUTTER

Makes: 450 g

YOU NEED

160 g raw almonds • 160 g raw Brazil nuts

½ teaspoon coconut oil • pinch of salt

10 minutes

Almonds are high in protein and calcium, while Brazil nuts are rich in selenium, which supports the immune system.

B *Builds bones* **H** *Heart support* **I** *Boosts immunity*

Blitz all of the ingredients for 8–10 minutes in a food processor until smooth and creamy. Stop the processor every few minutes to scrape down the sides. Use as a spread on toast or dip for vegetable sticks.

CRISPY TOFU

Serves: 2–3

YOU NEED

300 g silken tofu, cut into 3 cm cubes • 2 tablespoons light soy sauce

250 ml dashi stock (fish broth) • 1½ tablespoons mirin

7 g piece ginger, peeled and finely grated • 2 tablespoons potato starch

250 ml coconut oil • 1 spring onion, sliced on the diagonal

Tofu is a delicious, versatile plant-based protein that contains 8 essential amino acids and plenty of important minerals like iron, calcium and manganese.

A *Anti-ageing* **B** *Builds bones* **H** *Heart support*

Arrange the tofu cubes on kitchen paper and drain for 20 minutes. Gently heat the soy sauce, dashi stock, mirin and ginger. Keep warm. Sift the potato starch onto a plate and roll each tofu square until lightly coated, shaking off any excess. Set aside. Heat the oil to 170°C/338°F, or until a chunk of tofu turns golden in less than 1 minute when dropped in. Fry the tofu in batches until golden all over. Drain. Serve with the warm dressing and spring onions on top.

COCONUT GUACAMOLE

Serves: 4

YOU NEED
4 ripe avocados (about 450 g), stoned, peeled and roughly chopped
5 tablespoons fresh coconut meat, or equal amount of dried coconut rehydrated
in water for 20 minutes then drained • finely grated rind and juice of 2 limes
1 green chilli, deseeded and finely diced • ¼ teaspoon Tabasco sauce
pinch of salt • 10 g coriander leaves, chopped

Avocados are known for their healthy fat content, which stabilises cholesterol levels, while chilli is an excellent immunity booster, due to its heating effect on the body.

H *Heart support*   **I** *Fights infection*   **I** *Boosts immunity*

Mash all of the ingredients together with a fork until well combined, but still chunky. Chill until ready to serve.

BACON, BANANA & COCONUT BAGEL

Serves: 1

YOU NEED

1 teaspoon coconut oil • 1 banana, peeled and thickly sliced

1½ rashers rindless bacon (about 75 g) • 1 teaspoon maple syrup

1 bagel, cut in half and toasted

1 tablespoon unsweetened dried coconut, shredded

Bananas are high in potassium and dietary fibre, which keeps the digestive system healthy, and bacon is high in protein.

D *Aids digestion*   **B** *Brain support*   **B** *Blood cell formation*

Heat the oil in a pan over a medium heat and fry the banana slices until golden on both sides. Set aside. Wipe the pan clean and fry the bacon over a medium to high heat until crispy and golden. Turn off the heat and while the pan is hot, add the maple syrup and toss the bacon to coat. Arrange the banana slices evenly between the bagel halves, then gently crush and spread the banana over the bagels.
Tear the bacon into large pieces and arrange on top.
Scatter the coconut on top and serve.

POTATOES WITH COCONUT YOGHURT

Serves: 4

YOU NEED

4 medium baking potatoes (about 700 g), scrubbed, skin left on, each cut
into 5–6 slices • 2 garlic cloves, crushed • 1 teaspoon salt
10 g rosemary • 2 teaspoons coconut oil
2 teaspoons chipotle in adobo, crushed into a paste
100 g Coconut Yoghurt (see page 16)

Coconut yoghurt is an excellent source of beneficial probiotics that assist healthy digestion and a strong immune system.

P *Probiotics*   **D** *Aids digestion*   **I** *Boosts immunity*

Preheat the oven to 180°C/350°F/Gas 4. Place each potato in a double layer of foil. Crush the garlic with the salt into a paste using a mortar and pestle. Add the rosemary and crush. Add the oil and stir to combine. Divide the paste among the potatoes and coat well. Wrap and bake for 45 minutes until golden and soft. Mix the chipotle paste and yoghurt together. To serve, unwrap each potato and top with yoghurt.

BEETROOT CHIPS WITH FETA & MINT

Serves: 3–4

YOU NEED
4 medium beetroot (about 600 g), peeled and sliced into thin rounds
1 tablespoon coconut oil, melted • 1 teaspoon salt
60 g feta cheese, crumbled • 10 g mint leaves, finely chopped

Beetroot is full of antioxidants that cleanse the liver and are rich in dietary fibre. It also contains glutamine, an amino acid essential to the health of the intestinal tract.

F *High-fibre* **D** *Detoxifying* **L** *Cleanses liver*

Preheat the oven to 180°C/350°F/Gas 4. Line 2 baking trays with baking paper. Toss the beetroot with the oil and salt. Spread out in a single layer on trays. Place the baking paper over tray each and bake for 20 minutes until the edges start to dry out. Remove the baking paper, swap over the trays and bake for 10 minutes, removing the chips as they become lightened in colour. Transfer the chips to a wire rack to cool. Serve topped with mint and feta.

SWEET POTATO & LEEK QUESADILLA

Serves: 4

YOU NEED

1 sweet potato, peeled and grated • ½ leek (white part only), sliced

1 teaspoon chipotle in adobo sauce, finely minced to a paste

1 tablespoon coconut oil • 150 g mozzarella cheese, grated

juice of ½ lime • 4 corn tortillas • ½ teaspoon salt

30 minutes

Sweet potatoes are rich in vitamin A, antioxidants and fibre, which assist digestive
health and manages blood sugars.

F *High-fibre*   **A** *Anti-inflammatory*   **B** *Stabilises blood sugar*

Heat the oil in a pan and fry the leek for a few minutes. Add the sweet potato, salt
and chipotle paste and cook for a few minutes until the potato has softened. Add
the lime juice. Heat a frying pan. Lay a tortilla flat in the pan, spoon a quarter of
the mixture on one half, add a handful of mozzarella, then fold over the other half.
Dry-fry on one side until golden brown, then flip over and cook the other side.
Keep warm, and repeat with the rest of the tortillas.

LIME PRAWNS WITH MACADAMIA CRUMB

Serves: 1–2

YOU NEED

6 whole raw prawns, deveined and shelled, with tails intact, rinsed and pat dry

juice of 1 lime • 1 teaspoon coconut oil • 1 garlic clove, crushed

2 kaffir lime leaves, centre spine removed and thinly sliced

1 raw macadamia nut, finely grated

small pinch of salt

Prawns are high in zinc and protein and macadamias contain essential vitamins and minerals like manganese and copper, making it a filling, nutritious snack.

B *Bone building* **A** *Anti-inflammatory* **H** *Heart support*

Put the prawns in a bowl and cover with the lime juice. Chill for 10 minutes. Heat the oil in a frying pan over a medium to high heat, add the garlic and half of the kaffir lime leaves and fry for 30 seconds. Add the prawns and salt and toss to coat. Cook for 2–4 minutes until the prawns are golden all over. Serve the prawns with finely grated macadamia and the remaining kaffir lime leaves on top.

CHARGRILLED MISO CORN

Serves: 2

YOU NEED

2 corn cobs (about 330 g each), husks pulled down but left attached at the bottom

1 teaspoon coconut oil, plus extra for brushing • ½ garlic clove, crushed

3 teaspoons miso • 1 teaspoon tamarind paste • 1 teaspoon Dijon mustard

1 teaspoon parsley leaves, chopped

Miso is a fermented food so it contains nutritional probiotics, plenty of B vitamins and is a good source of plant-based protein.

P *Probiotic*   D *Aids digestion*   B *Blood sugar control*

Blanch the corn in boiling water for 3–4 minutes. Pat dry. Combine the coconut oil, garlic, miso, tamarind and mustard. Rub all over the corn. Brush a griddle pan with oil and put on a high heat. When the pan begins to smoke, add the corn and chargrill, turning, for about 8 minutes. Sprinkle with parsley.

SWEETS

Most of these sweets can be made ahead of time, stored in the fridge or freezer and then put together when needed, which means when unexpected friends 'drop in' you never have to go without dessert.

Salted Caramel Popcorn • Peppermint Chocolate
Balls • Coconut Brown Rice Pudding
Raspberry Cheesecake Jars
Orange & Cardamom Coconut Custard
Coconut, Ginger & Mint Granita

SALTED CARAMEL POPCORN

Serves: 4

YOU NEED

400 ml coconut cream • 100 g coconut sugar • 1½ teaspoons salt
1 tablespoon coconut oil • 120 g popcorn kernels

Coconut sugar comes from the nectar of the coconut palm blossom. It has a low glycaemic index (GI) and contains 12 amino acids and minerals.

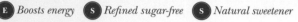

E *Boosts energy*   **S** *Refined sugar-free*   **S** *Natural sweetener*

Heat the coconut cream, sugar and ½ teaspoon of the salt gently for 50 minutes until thick and golden, stirring occasionally. Preheat the oven to 120°C/250°F/Gas ½. Line 2 baking trays with baking paper. Heat the oil in a pan over a medium heat. Drop in 2–3 kernels of corn, cover the pan and when the corn pops, add the remaining kernels. Cover. Leave on the heat until the popping stops. Spread the popcorn over trays in a single layer. Pour half of the caramel over to coat the popcorn. Bake for 45–50 minutes, stirring frequently. Sprinkle with the remaining salt and cool.

PEPPERMINT CHOCOLATE BALLS

Makes: about 18 balls

YOU NEED
160 g raw almonds • 165 g dried dates, soaked in hot water for 20 minutes
then drained • 30 g cacao powder • pinch of salt • 80 ml coconut oil, melted
5 drops pure peppermint oil • 25 g dried shredded coconut (unsweetened)

The combination of high-fibre dates and peppermint oil in these bliss balls
are a powerful aid to healthy digestion.

E *Energising*   **D** *Aids digestion*   **S** *Refined sugar-free*

Pulse all of the ingredients, except the coconut oil, peppermint oil and shredded
coconut, in a food processor until everything is combined and the nuts are finely
chopped. Add the oils and shredded coconut. Pulse until just combined. Scoop out
1 teaspoon of mixture at a time and roll into small balls. Freeze the balls for
20–25 minutes. Remove the balls from the freezer 5 minutes before eating.

COCONUT BROWN RICE PUDDING

Serves: 4

YOU NEED

1 litre canned or fresh coconut milk • 120 g brown rice

3 tablespoons coconut sugar • 1 teaspoon ground cinnamon, plus extra for dusting

1 teaspoon vanilla extract • ¼ teaspoon salt • 40 g raw pistachios, chopped

Brown rice is high in protein, while pistachios are rich in antioxidants and have plenty of health benefits for a healthy heart.

H *Heart support*   **A** *Antioxidants*   **C** *Lowers cholesterol*

Put all of the ingredients, except the pistachios, in a deep pan. Bring to the boil. Reduce the heat and simmer for 40 minutes, stirring occasionally, until all the liquid is absorbed and the rice is just cooked. Divide among bowls and top with pistachios and extra cinnamon.

RASPBERRY CHEESECAKE JARS

Serves: 4

YOU NEED
250 g crème fraîche • 60 ml coconut cream

2 tablespoons pure maple syrup • 1 teaspoon vanilla extract

100 g ginger biscuits • 120 g fresh or frozen raspberries

Raspberries contain high amounts of fibre, antioxidants, vitamins and minerals, in particular vitamin C, and folate, which give the immune system a boost.

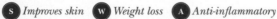

S *Improves skin*　**W** *Weight loss*　**A** *Anti-inflammatory*

Place all of the ingredients, except the biscuits and raspberries, in a large bowl and whisk to combine. Crumble half of each biscuit into the bottom of four 125 ml jars or bowls. Spoon in the cheesecake mixture until the jar is half full. Crumble the remaining biscuit on top, then divide the remaining cheesecake mixture among the jars. Sprinkle raspberries on top.

ORANGE & CARDAMOM COCONUT CUSTARD

Serves: 4

YOU NEED

400 ml canned or fresh coconut cream • 1 teaspoon cardamom seeds
rind of 1½ oranges, cut into thick strips • 4 egg yolks
60 g raw unrefined cane sugar • 3 tablespoons potato starch • ¼ teaspoon salt

Cardamom is rich in fibre that is known to significantly lower blood pressure.

D *Dairy-free*   **A** *Antidepressant*   **H** *Heart support*

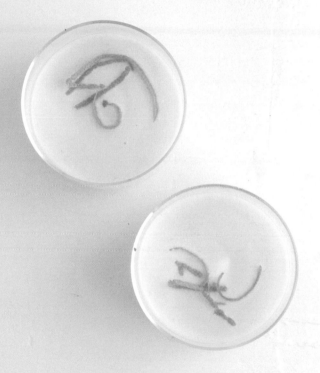

Heat the coconut cream, cardamom seeds and orange peel gently in a pan for 30 minutes, stirring occasionally. Remove from the heat just before it reaches boiling point. Strain through a sieve into a heatproof jug. Discard the seeds and orange peel. Whisk the egg yolks, sugar, potato starch and salt until light and foamy. Slowly add the coconut cream mixture and whisk until combined. Strain through a sieve into a pan. Cook over a medium to low heat, whisking, for 5–7 minutes until thick and creamy.

COCONUT, GINGER & MINT GRANITA

Serves: 6

YOU NEED
125 ml water • 120 g raw unrefined cane sugar

15 g piece ginger, peeled and thickly sliced • 400 ml canned or fresh coconut cream

15 g mint leaves, finely chopped, plus a few whole leaves to decorate

Coconut cream is high in good fats that boost metabolism and lower cholesterol, while mint is a cleansing herb known to soothe the digestive tract.

D *Aids digestion*   **I** *Infection fighting*   **M** *Boosts metabolism*

Boil the water, sugar and ginger for 2–3 minutes until the sugar dissolves. Cool completely, then remove the ginger. Pulse the coconut cream and ginger syrup into a blender and blitz for 30 seconds. Pour into a deep freezerproof tray and stir in the mint. Freeze for at least 6 hours, or overnight. Using a fork, scrape into crystals and freeze again until ready to eat. Decorate with mint leaves.

BAKING

These indulgent cakes, biscuits and muesli bars are nourishing treats as they contain the goodness of coconut oil and use natural sweeteners. For added nutrients substitute coconut flour for plain flour – use 40 g for every 160 g of plain flour.

Coconut & Lime Crème Brûlée • Carrot
Cupcakes with Coconut Icing
Mini Lemon & Coconut Oil Cakes • Coffee & Fig
Pound Cake • Coconut Anzac Biscuits
Coconut & Cranberry Pudding • Chai Spice
Coconut Crumble • Chocolate & Coconut Bars
Salted Chocolate Fondants

COCONUT & LIME CRÈME BRÛLÉE

Makes: 6

YOU NEED

550 ml canned or fresh coconut cream

1 vanilla pod, split lengthways and seeds scraped out • 2 kaffir lime leaves

5 egg yolks • 2 tablespoons coconut sugar, plus extra for dusting

40 g raw honey • 1½ teaspoons agar agar powder or 5 g gelatine powder

Egg yolks are densely nutritious and contain over 80% of the vitamins and minerals found in a whole egg. They are rich in iron, potassium and folate.

B *Builds bones*   **G** *Gluten-free*   **H** *Heart support*

Preheat the oven to 140°C/275°F/Gas 1. Boil the cream, vanilla and kaffir lime leaves, whisking. Strain. Whisk the yolks, sugar, honey and agar until the sugar dissolves and the mixture is thick, about 2 minutes. Gradually add the hot cream, whisking. Strain the custard and pour into 6 × 200 ml ramekins, filling almost to the top. Put the ramekins in a tin and pour in enough hot water to come halfway up the sides of the ramekins. Bake for 50–60 minutes until just set, but with a slight wobble. Chill for 2 hours until set. Preheat the grill to high. Lightly dust the tops of the crème brûlées with sugar. Grill for 1–2 minutes until the sugar caramelises.

CARROT CUPCAKES WITH COCONUT ICING

Makes: 10–12 cakes

YOU NEED

2 tablespoons (50 g) canned or fresh coconut cream • 2 carrots, grated

250 g plain flour, sifted • 2 teaspoons baking powder

80 g coconut oil • 3 eggs • 4 tablespoons (100 g) maple syrup

Icing

250 ml canned or fresh coconut cream (if using canned don't shake or tip can to

encourage separation) • 1 tablespoon (25 g) maple syrup

Carrots are a rich source of vitamin A and coconut oil is full of good fats
that the body needs for optimum health.

E *Eye protection*   **H** *Heart support*   **S** *Refined-sugar-free*

Chill the coconut cream for the icing in a bowl overnight. Preheat the oven to
200°C/400°F/Gas 6. Line a 12-hole muffin tin with paper cases. Whisk the eggs, oil
and maple syrup until fluffy, about 3–4 minutes. Gradually add the cream, carrot,
flour and baking powder and whisk until just combined. Divide the batter among
the cases. Bake for 25–30 minutes until golden and a skewer inserted into the centre
comes out clean. Cool in the tin. For the icing, combine the chilled cream and
maple syrup in a chilled bowl and whisk until stiff peaks form.
Spread the cupcakes with icing and serve.

MINI LEMON & COCONUT OIL CAKES

Makes: 16

YOU NEED

juice and rind of 3 large lemons (about 250 ml) • 250 ml milk • 300 g plain flour,
sifted • 150 g coconut sugar • 80 g coconut oil, plus extra for oiling
3 eggs • 20 g baking powder

Coconut oil is full of cholesterol-lowering good fats, while the lemon juice in these cakes balances the richness of the oil and adds vitamin C.

S *Refined-sugar-free* **I** *Fights infection* **C** *Lowers cholesterol*

Preheat oven to 180°C/350°F/Gas 4. Lightly oil two 12-hole mini cake tins. Whisk the sugar, eggs and oil until fluffy, about 3–4 minutes. Gradually add the milk, lemon juice and rind and whisk until combined. Add the flour and baking powder and mix briefly with an electric whisk on low speed until just combined. Divide the batter among tins, leaving a 1 cm gap for expansion. Bake for 12–15 minutes until golden and a skewer comes out clean when inserted in centre.

COFFEE & FIG POUND CAKE

Makes: 1 loaf cake

YOU NEED

110 ml ready-made strong coffee • 1 tablespoon blackstrap molasses or treacle
5 eggs • 150 g coconut oil • 110 g coconut sugar, plus extra for dusting
330 g plain flour • 200 g dried figs, stalks removed and roughly chopped,
soaked in warm water for 20 minutes then drained

Blackstrap molasses contains vital vitamins and minerals for healthy blood, bones and the immune system, such as calcium, magnesium and selenium.

B *Builds bones* **I** *Boosts immunity* **H** *Improves hair quality*

Preheat the oven to 160°C/325°F/Gas 3. Line a 21 × 10 cm loaf tin with baking paper. Heat the coffee and molasses gently until well combined. Cool completely. Beat the eggs, oil and sugar until light and fluffy. Slowly add the coffee mixture and combine. Sift in the flour and mix until smooth. Pour half of the batter into the tin. Sprinkle half of the figs over, then add the remaining batter. Top with the remaining figs, sprinkle with extra sugar and bake for 1 hour 20 minutes until cooked when tested with a skewer. Cool in the tin for 5 minutes. Turn out onto a wire rack to cool completely before serving.

COCONUT ANZAC BISCUITS

Makes: about 16 biscuits

YOU NEED

225 g ground almonds • 135 g rolled oats • 60 g dried coconut chips
55 g coconut flour • 60 ml maple syrup • 110 g coconut oil
½ teaspoon bicarbonate of soda • 1 tablespoon hot water

Ground almonds and coconut flour are high in protein, while oats contain beneficial fibre and have cholesterol-lowering properties.

(F) *High-fibre*   (A) *Anti-inflammatory*   (C) *Lowers cholesterol*

Preheat the oven to 130°C/266°F/Gas 1. Line a baking tray with baking paper. Combine the almonds, oats, coconut chips and flour. Heat the maple syrup and oil gently. Combine the bicarbonate of soda and water, add to the maple syrup misture and stir. Add the wet ingredients to the dry ingredients and mix. Add some water to help the mixture stick together if necessary. Roll 1 tablespoon of the mixture into a small ball. Press onto a tray and flatten slightly. Repeat. Bake for 50–60 minutes until golden. Cool in the oven for 5 minutes, then cool on a wire rack.

COCONUT & CRANBERRY PUDDING

Serves: 4

YOU NEED

5 slices of good-quality sourdough (about 220 g), halved on the diagonal

2 tablespoons coconut oil • 4 egg yolks • 75 g coconut sugar

600 ml coconut cream • 1 tablespoon lemon juice • 1 teaspoon lemon zest

50 g dried cranberries, soaked in warm water for 20 minutes then drained

The fermentation of sourdough breaks down the starches in grains, leaving us with a bread that is gentler on the digestive system.

D *Aids digestion*   **I** *Boosts immunity*   **H** *Heart support*

Preheat the oven to 180°C/350°F/Gas 4. Heat a griddle pan. Spread the sourdough with 1 tablespoon of the oil and chargrill for 1 minute each side. Oil a small baking dish with the remaining oil and arrange the sourdough snugly in a dish. Whisk together the egg yolks and sugar until fluffy. Heat the cream, lemon juice and zest until just about to boil, remove and slowly add to the egg, whisking. Pour over the bread and leave to soak for 20 minutes. Put the dish in a roasting tray. Pour in boiling water until it reaches halfway up the dish. Scatter the cranberries over. Bake for 40–45 minutes until custard is just set. Cool for 5 minutes.

CHAI SPICE COCONUT CRUMBLE

Serves: 4

YOU NEED
80 ml water • 1 teaspoon ground sweet garam masala • 80 g coconut sugar
4 ripe pears (about 400 g), peeled, cored and cut into chunks

Topping
130 g rolled oats • 50 g coconut sugar • 2 tablespoons coconut oil, melted
30 g dried coconut chips • 40 g salted pistachios, shelled and roughly chopped

Oats are a great plant-based protein and source of iron, plus the spices in the garam masala contain vitamins and minerals that strengthen the immune system.

E *Energising* **F** *High-fibre* **I** *Boosts immunity*

Preheat the oven to 200°C/400°F/Gas 6. Line a baking tray with baking paper. Spread the oats for the topping onto the tray and toast in the oven for 10 minutes. Cool completely. Boil the water, garam masala and sugar together, then add the pears and simmer gently for a few minutes. Remove from the heat and spoon the filling into 4 small ovenproof dishes. Combine all the topping ingredients, including the oats, then sprinkle over the fruit. Bake for 25–30 minutes until the pears are cooked and the crumble topping is golden.

CHOCOLATE & COCONUT BARS

Makes: about 12 bars

YOU NEED

130 g rolled oats • 30 g puffed rice cereal • 70 g dried coconut chips
190 g brown rice syrup • 300 g dried dates, chopped to a paste, soaked in warm
water for 20 minutes then drained • finely grated rind of 2 oranges
120 g dark chocolate (at least 70% cocoa solids), broken into pieces

These muesli bars are a perfect on-the-go energy boost. The oats and dates are good sources of fibre and improve digestion.

F *High-fibre*   **E** *Energising*   **D** *Aids digestion*

Preheat the oven to 175°C/347°F/Gas 4. Line an 18 × 28 cm baking tray with baking paper. Toast the oats in the oven for 8–10 minutes. Cool. Combine the rice cereal, coconut and oats. Pour the rice syrup and dates over the dry mixture and mix, breaking up any clumps. Pour the mixture into the tray and press into a flat, even layer. Melt the chocolate and orange rind in a heatproof bowl set over a pan of simmering water. Drizzle the chocolate on top of the coconut bars. Chill before cutting.

SALTED CHOCOLATE FONDANTS

Makes: 8

YOU NEED

5 eggs • 5 egg yolks • 125 g unrefined sugar • 225 g coconut oil, plus extra for oiling

225 g dark chocolate (at least 70% cocoa solids), broken into pieces

1 teaspoon salt • 50 g plain flour

40 g dried cranberries, soaked in water for 20 minutes then drained

Cranberries are packed with vitamins and minerals, particularly vitamins C, E and K, which help to build the immune system and lower blood pressure.

A *Anti-inflammatory*   **I** *Boosts immunity*   **B** *Lowers blood pressure*

Oil 8 × 200 ml moulds. Whisk the eggs, yolks and sugar for 5–6 minutes until pale and frothy. Melt the oil, chocolate and salt in a heatproof bowl set over a pan of simmering water. Add to the egg mixture, whisk to combine and fold in the flour. Divide among the moulds. Drop 6–8 cranberries into the centre of each fondant, poking down with a skewer. Chill until firm. Preheat the oven to 180°C/350°F/Gas 4. Bake for 20–25 minutes until risen but with gooey centres. Serve hot.

BEAUTY

These quick DIY beauty recipes reveal the healing and medicinal properties of coconut oil. Commercial beauty products can be full of chemicals, so making your own natural treatments is well worth the effort.

Hair Wrap • Moisturising Face Mask
Antioxidant Face Scrub • Body Scrub
Detoxifying 'Oil Pulling' Mouthwash

HAIR WRAP

Makes: 1 treatment

YOU NEED

1 teaspoon fresh rosemary leaves • 2 tablespoons coconut oil

Coconut oil acts as a conditioner to nourish dry hair, while the oil from the rosemary soothes the scalp and stimulates hair follicles making hair grow stronger.

H *Repairs hair* **S** *Scalp health* **A** *Anti-inflammatory*

Crush the rosemary in a mortar and pestle to release the oils. Add the coconut oil and stir to combine. Massage the mixture into the scalp and roots of the hair, working your way down to the ends to completely coat the hair. Leave for 20 minutes, or overnight for damaged hair. Rinse and shampoo and condition as usual. The treatment can be stored in the refrigerator for 1 week.

MOISTURISING FACE MASK

Makes: 1 treatment

YOU NEED

2 tablespoons raw organic honey • 1 tablespoon coconut oil

2 teaspoons coconut flour • 1 teaspoon lemon juice

¼ teaspoon fresh or dried organic (unsprayed) lavender blossoms

(available from health food stores/farmers' markets)

Lavender soothes skin irritations and is a gentle cleanser. Coconut oil provides skin with an important moisture barrier, while raw honey cleans and protects.

S *Soothes skin*   **M** *Moisturising*   **A** *Antibacterial*

Combine the ingredients in a bowl. Set aside. Wash your face and pat dry. Spread the face mask evenly across the face and neck, avoiding the eyes. Leave for 5–10 minutes. Wash off completely. Dry face and moisturise as usual. The treatment can be stored in the refrigerator for 2–3 days.

ANTIOXIDANT FACE SCRUB

Makes: 1 treatment

YOU NEED
40 g blueberries • ½ teaspoon ground cinnamon
½ teaspoon ground nutmeg • ¼ teaspoon ground fenugreek
1 tablespoon coconut oil

Nutmeg has powerful antibacterial properties that clear skin blemishes and reduce marks caused by acne. The antioxidants in blueberries nourish and cleanse the skin.

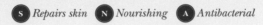

S *Repairs skin* **N** *Nourishing* **A** *Antibacterial*

Mash the blueberries with a fork. Add the spices and coconut oil and stir to combine. Wash face and pat dry, leaving it lightly damp. Apply face mask in a generous, even layer, covering face, neck and décolletage area. Leave for 15 minutes, then rinse off with warm water using gentle circular motions. Dry face and moisturise. Use the scrub on the same day.

BODY SCRUB

Makes: 1 treatment

YOU NEED

170 g rolled oats • 2 tablespoons raw organic honey

2 tablespoons coconut oil

Both coconut oil and honey have powerful antibacterial properties when used on the skin. Oats are known to condition and repair damaged skin cells.

S *Repairs skin* **C** *Repairs cells* **A** *Antibacterial*

Pulse all of the ingredients in a food processor for 1–2 minutes until just combined. Put in a bowl. Scoop small amounts of scrub into your hand and spread over your entire body, using gentle circular motions. Rinse off immediately with warm water. Dry and moisturise as usual. Use the scrub on the same day.

DETOXIFYING 'OIL PULLING' MOUTHWASH

Makes: 1 treatment

YOU NEED

1 tablespoon coconut oil, melted

Oil pulling is an ancient Ayurvedic technique to draw out toxins from the body and improve oral health.

(D) *Detoxifying* (M) *Mouth-cleansing* (A) *Antibacterial*

Swirl the coconut oil in your mouth for 20 minutes, 'pushing' and 'pulling' it through your teeth, until oil turns milky white, indicating it has 'pulled' bacteria from between the teeth. Spit out the oil. Rinse your mouth thoroughly with water and brush and floss as usual.

INDEX

Acknowledgements

For my friends in Sri Lanka, who generously shared their time and
their kitchens and introduced me to coconut oil.

For Laalimaa, my 'blushing sky', who slept so soundly while I worked
on these recipes. You are the umami of life.

Coconut Oil by Jessica Oldfield

First published in 2016 by Hachette Books
(Marabout)
This English hardback edition published in
2016 by Hardie Grant Books

Hardie Grant Books (UK)
52-54 Southwark Street
London SE1 1UN
hardiegrant.co.uk

Hardie Grant Books (Australia)
Ground Floor, Building 1
658 Church Street
Melbourne, VIC 3121
hardiegrant.com.au

The moral rights of Jessica Oldfield to be
identified as the author of this work have
been asserted by her in accordance with the
Copyright, Designs and Patents Act 1988.

Text © Jessica Oldfield
Photography © Victoria Wall Harris

British Library Cataloguing-in-Publication
Data. A catalogue record for this book is
available from the British Library.

ISBN: 978-1-78488-069-9

Publisher: Catie Ziller
Author: Jessica Oldfield
Designer and illustrator: Alice Chadwick
Photographer: Victoria Wall Harris
Food Stylist: Anna Shillinglaw Hampton
Editor: Kathy Steer

For the English hardback edition:
Publisher: Kate Pollard
Senior Editor: Kajal Mistry
Editorial Assistant: Hannah Roberts
Cover image: iStock
Cover Design: Hardie Grant Books
Colour Reproduction by p2d

Printed and bound in China by 1010

10 9 8 7 6 5 4 3 2 1